Maya Moore

MAYO
CLINIC
23

THE STORY OF THE MINNESOTA LYNX

Aerial Powers

WNBA: A HISTORY OF WOMEN'S HOOPS

THE STORY OF THE

MINNESOTA
LYNX

JIM WHITING

Katie Smith

CREATIVE EDUCATION / CREATIVE PAPERBACKS

Published by Creative Education and Creative Paperbacks
P.O. Box 227, Mankato, Minnesota 56002
Creative Education and Creative Paperbacks are imprints of
The Creative Company
www.thecreativecompany.us

Design and production by Blue Design (www.bluedes.com)
Art direction by Rita Marshall

Photographs by Getty (Julio Aguilar, Leon Bennett, David Berding, Steph
Chambers, Tim Clayton/Corbis, Kevin C. Cox, Hannah Foslien, Harry How,
Icon Sportswire, Mitchell Layton, Doug Pensinger, Star Tribune)

Library of Congress Cataloging-in-Publication Data
Names: Whiting, Jim, 1943- author.
Title: The story of the Minnesota Lynx / by Jim Whiting.
Description: Mankato, Minnesota : Creative Education and Creative
    Paperbacks, [2024] | Series: Creative Sports. WNBA : A History of
    Women's Hoops. | Includes index. | Audience: Ages 8-12 | Audience:
    Grades 4-6 | Summary: "Middle grade basketball fans are introduced to
    the extraordinary history of WNBA's Minnesota Lynx with a photo-laden
    narrative of their greatest successes and losses"-- Provided by
    publisher.
Identifiers: LCCN 2022034249 (print) | LCCN 2022034250 (ebook) | ISBN
    9781640267237 (library binding) | ISBN 9781682772799 (paperback) | ISBN
    9781640008748 (pdf)
Subjects: LCSH: Minnesota Lynx (Basketball team)--History--Juvenile
    literature.
Classification: LCC GV885.52.M563 W55 2023 (print) | LCC GV885.52.M563
    (ebook) | DDC 796.323/6409776--dc23/eng/20220720
LC record available at https://lccn.loc.gov/2022034249
LC ebook record available at https://lccn.loc.gov/2022034250

Printed in China

Seimone Augustus

CONTENTS

LEGENDS OF THE HARDWOOD

Monica Wright

FROM DOORMAT TO DOMINANT

The Minnesota Lynx faced the Atlanta Dream in the 2011 Women's National Basketball Association (WNBA) Finals. In the previous season, Minnesota had a 13–21 record. Only one team was worse. Now, after one of the greatest single-season turnarounds in pro sports history, the Lynx were playing for the WNBA title. Minnesota won the first two games of the best-of-five series. Atlanta took a four-point halftime lead in Game 3. The Lynx held the Dream to just eight points in the third quarter. Minnesota scored 19 points themselves. Now they led 52–45. Atlanta didn't fold. They sank a three-point shot with 1:17 left in the game. That cut the Minnesota lead to a single point. Minnesota didn't fold either. The Lynx made nine free throws in the following minute. Former University of Minnesota standout guard Lindsay Whalen sank the final one. It made the score 73–67 and iced the game. The Lynx were WNBA champions!

That championship seemed unlikely after the way the team had played in its

KATIE SMITH
GUARD/SMALL FORWARD
HEIGHT: 5-FOOT-11
LYNX SEASONS: 1999–2005

MAKING AN IMPACT

Katie Smith was the Gatorade National High School Player of the Year in 1992. She starred at Ohio State University. Then she played three years in the American Basketball League (ABL). Smith joined the Lynx when the ABL folded. She had a modest start in her first season. She averaged 11.7 points per game. Then Smith became the team's primary outside shooting threat. During the next six seasons, she averaged more than 18 points per game. She was named to the All-WNBA First or Second Team four years in a row. Smith played in five All-Star Games. In 2006, she was named to the WNBA All-Decade Team. It honored the 10 players who had the greatest impact on the WNBA during the league's first 10 years.

first 12 seasons. It had joined the WNBA in 1999, two years after the league's founding. Minnesota had just two winning seasons during that time. Both times their record was barely over .500.

When Minnesota joined the WNBA, each of the league's teams was closely connected to the National Basketball Association (NBA) team in the same city. To emphasize those connections, WNBA teams adopted nicknames associated with their NBA partners. Minnesota's NBA team was the Timberwolves. Officials of the new WNBA franchise selected Lynx. Both animals are powerful predators that roam the Minnesota forests in search of prey.

The Lynx defeated the Detroit Shock, 68–51, in their first game. Well over halfway through the schedule, the Lynx were two games above .500, at 12–10. They won just 3 of the final 10 games. They finished 15–17. It wasn't good enough for the playoffs.

Nearly halfway through the 2000 season, the Lynx were 10–5. Then they lost eight in a row. They won five of the final nine games to once again finish at 15–17. They missed the playoffs again.

Unlike their first two seasons, the Lynx struggled at the start of the 2001 season. They were 5–5 after 10 games. But then they had two five-game losing streaks. Minnesota finished 12–20. Guard Katie Smith averaged 23.1 points per game. She was the league's leading scorer.

Things got even worse in 2002. The Lynx opened with four wins in the first seven games. Then they had a five-game losing streak. After two wins, they dropped the next seven games. They finished 10–22, last in the conference.

MODEST SUCCESSES

Minnesota's luck changed in 2003. The team persuaded five-time Olympian and four-time gold medalist Teresa Edwards to come out of retirement and provide veteran leadership. The Lynx head coach, Suzie McConnell-Serio, had been a teammate with Edwards on two Olympic teams. At age 38, Edwards was the oldest rookie in WNBA history. Minnesota had a seven-game winning streak during the season. They also avoided long losing streaks. They finished 18–16. It was their first winning season and first time in the playoffs. They faced the Los Angeles Sparks in the conference semifinals. The Sparks were favored. They opened up a 21-point lead in the second half of Game 1. The Lynx clawed their way back. With less than 10 seconds remaining, the score was tied at 72–72. Lynx forward Tamika Williams stole an inbounds pass. She scored the winning basket. It was the league's largest second-half playoff comeback. The win also broke a 16-game losing streak to the Sparks. Los Angeles came back to win the next two games in the best-of-three series.

It seemed that the Lynx had found a winning combination. After opening 7–9 in 2004, they had a six-game winning streak. Again they finished at 18–16 and made the playoffs. This time the Seattle Storm swept the conference semifinals.

In 2005, the Lynx were at 11–9 more than halfway through the season. But a mid-season trade with Detroit for Smith took away the team's best offensive weapon. They finished with a 14–20 mark.

Val Whiting-Raymond

There was a silver lining. Minnesota's poor record gave them the top overall choice in the 2006 WNBA Draft. They chose All-American forward/guard Seimone Augustus of Louisiana State University. Augustus scored 21 points in her first game. Soon afterward, she scored 26 as the Lynx crushed the Sparks, 114–71. It was a league scoring record at the time. But Minnesota couldn't build on that momentum. They had losing streaks of five and six games and finished 10–24. Augustus set a still-standing rookie scoring record of 21.9 points per game. She was an obvious choice for WNBA Rookie of the Year.

innesota lost the first seven games of the 2007 season. During the season they had a 10-game losing streak. The Lynx finished with a repeat of the previous season's 10–24 mark.

The 2008 season began full of promise. Minnesota won its first five games. Then they faded, hovering around the .500 mark for the rest of the season. They finished 16–18. One bright spot was guard Candice Wiggins. She averaged nearly 16 points per game. She was named to the WNBA All-Rookie Team and honored as the WNBA Sixth Woman of the Year.

Minnesota had a good start in the 2009 season. They were 7–3 after 10 games. They struggled the rest of the way. They ended the season by losing 8 of their final 11. Their final record was just 14–20.

The Lynx had had losing seasons in 9 of its 11 years and just a single playoff victory during that time. No one could have foreseen what was about to happen to the limping franchise.

SEIMONE AUGUSTUS
FORWARD/GUARD
HEIGHT: 6-FOOT-0
LYNX SEASONS: 2006–19

HIGH EXPECTATIONS

Seimone Augustus was on the cover of *Sports Illustrated for Women* magazine in 1998 with the question, "Is She the Next Michael Jordan?" She was an eighth grader at the time. She was named a McDonald's High School All-American in 2002. She led Louisiana State University to three Final Four appearances. As a junior and senior, Augustus was named College Player of the Year. She started every game during her career with the Lynx, except for 2019, when she was injured. She averaged nearly 16 points a game. Augustus was named to the All-WNBA First or Second Teams six times. She played in eight All-Star Games. In 2021, Augustus was named to The W25. It honored the 25 players with the greatest impact on the league in its first 25 years. The following year she became the first LSU female athlete with a statue on the school's campus.

MINNESOTA LYNX

LEGENDS
OF THE HARDWOOD

Cheryl Reeve

**CHERYL REEVE
HEAD COACH
LYNX SEASONS:
2010–PRESENT**

WHAT A COACH!

Cheryl Reeve was a standout guard for La Salle University in the mid-1980s. Her coaching career began as a La Salle assistant after she graduated. She became head coach at Indiana State University in 1995. Six years later, she joined the Charlotte Sting as an assistant coach. She also had stints with the Cleveland Rockers and the Detroit Shock. "She really learned the in's and out's of being a professional coach," said longtime basketball reporter Mechelle Voepel, "which is different than being a college coach." Reeve became the Lynx coach in 2010. The team won just 13 games that season. Eleven straight winning seasons followed. That stretch included four WNBA championships and three WNBA Coach of the Year honors.

REEVE TO THE RESCUE!

Minnesota hired Cheryl Reeve as coach before the 2010 season. "We're very excited about her passion and enthusiasm for the job, her lengthy experience as a coach, and her knowledge of the teams and the players in this league," said team executive Roger Griffith. The team traded for Lindsay Whalen before the season. She averaged nearly 13 points and 6 assists per game. They also signed veteran forward Rebekkah Brunson. She pulled down more than 10 rebounds per game. But Wiggins and Augustus were injured. The Lynx lost 9 of their first 11 games. They finished 13–21. Reeve blamed herself. "We are a bad basketball team," she said. "It starts at the top."

Once again Minnesota had the top overall selection in the WNBA Draft. Once again they struck gold. They selected University of Connecticut forward Maya Moore. She had twice been named as the College Player of the Year. In addition, Augustus and Wiggins had recovered from their injuries. Minnesota got off to yet another fast start. They won five games in a row after an opening loss. This time there would be no falling back. The Lynx had additional winning streaks of six and nine games. They had a league-best 27–7 mark. Moore joined Whalen, Brunson, and Augustus to form the "Core Four" of the Lynx. Moore averaged more than 13 points a game. She was named WNBA Rookie of the Year and played in the All-Star Game.

The Lynx faced San Antonio in the first round of the playoffs. Whalen tipped away a Silver Stars inbounds pass with four seconds left in Game 1 to give Minnesota a 66–65 win. San Antonio won Game 2. The Lynx won the deciding Game 3, 85–67. They easily swept Phoenix in the conference finals. Then they swept the Dream for their first championship! "The first person I went to hug was Seimone," Wiggins said. "We were together during those struggling years of the Lynx. Throughout our conflicts and camaraderie, the good and the bad, to have that moment, this is the beauty and power of sport."

innesota opened the 2012 season with 10 wins in a row. They had an 11-game streak later in the season. Again they finished 27–7. They calmed the Seattle Storm and doused the Sparks in the playoffs. But they couldn't cure the Indiana Fever. Indiana won the championship series, 3 games to 1.

Minnesota had another 10-game winning streak during the 2013 season. They finished 26–8. They were perfect in the playoffs, beating the Storm and the Mercury in two games each time and the Dream in three games. It was their second WNBA title in three years. "I'm sorry if we make it look easy, but it's very hard to get back here," said Augustus after the 86–77 championship-clinching victory. "We're just lucky to be in this position."

Rebekkah Brunson

INDIANA AT MINNESOTA
AUGUST 18, 2017

Sylvia Fowles

PREYING ON THE FEVER

Twelve days earlier, the Fever had defeated Minnesota,
84–82. No one could have foreseen the epic turnaround that
followed. Minnesota pounded Indiana, 111–52. The 59-point
difference is the largest margin of victory in WNBA history.
During a 13-minute stretch in the first half, the Lynx scored
37 unanswered points. That is also a league record. The
stretch began when the Lynx led 22–9. It ended with an
almost incomprehensible 59–9 lead. The epic beatdown was
especially remarkable because Minnesota played without
two key players, Lindsay Whalen and Rebekka Brunson. Sylvia
Fowles had 25 points to lead five other teammates in double
figures. "[The Lynx] were able to do anything they wanted
after about 90 seconds," said Fever coach Pokey Chatman.
"We never, ever came close to recovering."

TWO MORE TITLES

The Lynx opened the 2014 season with a seven-game winning streak. Late in the season, they ran off 11 straight to finish 25–9. They won two close games against San Antonio in the conference semifinals. But the Mercury took two out of three in the conference finals.

Minnesota added a key component during the 2015 season by trading for two-time WNBA Defensive Player of the Year Sylvia Fowles. Even though they didn't have any long winning streaks in 2015, they finished 22–12. They knocked off the Sparks in three games in the conference semifinals and the Mercury in two games in the conference finals. They faced the Fever in the WNBA Finals. It turned out to be a close series. The Fever won Game 1 by six points. The Lynx won Game 2 by six points and Game 3 by three. After another Fever six-point win, the Lynx easily won the deciding Game 5, 69–52. "This never gets old. Kinda coming to the microphone, champagne-soaked," said Coach Reeve to the happy home crowd.

The Lynx began 2016 with a 13-game winning streak. They finished it by winning seven of their last eight for a 28–6 finish. It was their best record yet. The playoff format had changed. The top eight teams qualified, regardless of conference. Minnesota's record gave them byes in the first two rounds. Each consisted of a single game. They swept the Mercury in the best-of-five league semifinals. They split the first four games with the Sparks in the WNBA Finals.

Sylvia Fowles

Game 5 came down to the closing seconds. A Moore jump shot put Minnesota ahead by a point with 14 seconds remaining. But the Sparks scored after snagging a rebound with 3.1 seconds left. They won the series.

Minnesota was almost as good in 2017. Several winning streaks gave them a 27–7 record. Once again they had two first-round byes in the playoffs. They swept the Washington Mystics in the league semifinals and faced the Sparks for the league title. Los Angeles won Game 1 by a single point. Minnesota evened the series with a 70–68 win in Game 2. Los Angeles won Game 3. The Lynx won Game 4. They seemed to have Game 5 well in hand. They led 79–69 with a minute and a half left. The Sparks stormed back with seven unanswered points. Moore put the game away with a shot over several defenders. The Lynx won 85–76 for their fourth WNBA title. It tied the Houston Comets for the most league championships. "I think every time you do this, it gets a little more special because it gets a little harder," Whalen said.

Maya Moore

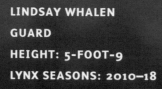

LINDSAY WHALEN
GUARD
HEIGHT: 5-FOOT-9
LYNX SEASONS: 2010–18

HOMETOWN HEROINE
RETURNS HOME

Lindsay Whalen is almost certainly the greatest female player in the history of the University of Minnesota. Lynx fans hoped she would stay home for her pro career. The Connecticut Sun had the fourth pick in the 2004 WNBA Draft. That was two spots higher than Minnesota. The Sun took Whalen. From that time on, Minnesota officials tried to get her back. The Lynx were finally able to trade for Whalen in 2010. Coach Cheryl Reeve was thrilled. "The expectation for this basketball team from day one [after Whalen's arrival] is going to be to win the Western Conference and compete for the WNBA Final." Her prediction proved to be perfect. The Lynx were WNBA champions in 2011. During her Lynx career, Whalen was named All-WNBA First or Second Team four times. She played in four All-Star Games. When she retired, she became the head women's coach at the University of Minnesota.

ALL GOOD THINGS MUST COME TO AN END

A ge finally began slowing down the Minnesota juggernaut in 2018. Augustus was 34. Whalen was 36. So was Brunson. They were still playing at a high level. But their best years were behind them. The Lynx spent the first part of the season below .500. A seven-game winning streak helped them finish with an overall 18–16 mark. They faced the Sparks in the playoffs. This time the teams met in the single-game first round. The Sparks won. It was just the second time in eight years that Minnesota wasn't in the WNBA Finals. Moore, Whalen, and Brunson left after the season. Augustus would be gone after the following season. The Core Four was no more.

Late in 2019, the Lynx were under .500 again. They were hampered by injuries and incorporating new players into the system. They managed to win five of the last six games to finish 18–16. Forward Napheesa Collier averaged more than 16 points a game. She was named WNBA Rookie of the Year. The Lynx faced the Storm in the first round. Seattle won 84–74.

The COVID-19 pandemic forced the league to start late in 2020 and shortened the season to 22 games. Minnesota finished 14–8. They had a first-round bye. They faced the Mercury in the second round. Earlier that day, guard Crystal Dangerfield had become the first WNBA second-round draft choice named WNBA Rookie of the Year. She celebrated by scoring 17 points. The Lynx won 80–79. Seattle swept them in three games in the league semifinals.

MAYA MOORE
FORWARD
HEIGHT: 6-FOOT-0
LYNX SEASONS: 2011–18

MAKING HER MARK ON AND OFF THE COURT

Sports Illustrated magazine noted that Maya Moore is "the greatest winner in the history of women's basketball." Back-to-back college national championships. Two Olympic gold medals. Four WNBA titles. All-WNBA First or Second Team seven times. WNBA Most Valuable Player (MVP). Many people were stunned when she chose not to play in the 2019 season when she was at the peak of her career. She wanted to work to make changes in the criminal justice system. She was especially concerned about the case of a man whom she believed had been wrongfully convicted when he was just 16. He had served many years in prison. Her efforts helped exonerate him in 2020. They were married soon afterward. *Time Magazine* named her as one of The 100 Most Influential People of 2020.

Napheesa Collier

The Lynx began 2021 with four losses. They finally surpassed the .500 level halfway through the season during an eight-game winning streak. They finished with 9 wins in the final 10 games for an overall 22–10 record. Fowles was named WNBA Defensive Player of the Year. Minnesota had a first-round bye. The Chicago Sky beat them in the second round.

The Lynx won just 3 of their first 13 games in 2022. They managed to claw back to playoff contention with two games left. They lost both to finish 14–22 and miss the playoffs. It was Reeve's first losing season in 12 years. Collier missed all but the last four games of the season due to the birth of her child. Several new players had problems fitting in. Former All-Star Angel McCoughtry played just two games. Fowles retired. She played the final eight years of her career in Minnesota. It is hard to find a player with more accomplishments: two WNBA titles, four Olympic gold medals, four Defensive Player of the Year awards, eight All-Star appearances. She is the league's all-time leader in rebounds, with 4,007. Reeve called her "The best-all-time classic center in the history of our league." "Better than 99 percent of players that have ever played," added All-Star teammate Maya Moore. Fowles made one of the most interesting post-WNBA career choices: mortician. That is a person who takes care of dead bodies and arranges for their funerals.

The Minnesota Lynx got off to a slow start after joining the WNBA in 1999. They won just a single playoff game in their first 12 seasons. Then Minnesota became what is almost certainly the league's dominant team. Lynx fans expect them to continue to contend for league titles in the coming years.

Kayla McBride

INDEX